Contents

IN THE BOUNDLESS OCEAN OF SPACE, EVERY STAR IS A BEACON OF WONDER, GUIDING OUR CURIOSITY TO SAIL BEYOND THE HORIZONS OF IMAGINATION.

Thank you for your support, I hope you enjoy the book.

Mercury

Distance from the Sun: Mercury is about 57.9 million kilometers (36 million miles) away from the Sun.

Average Temperature: Mercury's temperatures can range from -173°C (-280°F) at night to 427°C (800°F) during the day due to its lack of atmosphere.

Size: Mercury has a diameter of approximately 4,880 kilometers (3,032 miles).

Orbital Period: Mercury completes an orbit around the Sun in about 88 Earth days.

Gravity: Mercury's gravity is about 38% of Earth's, meaning if you weigh 100 kg on Earth, you would weigh 38 kg on Mercury.

Mercury is a fascinating planet and it's the closest one to the Sun in our solar system. Imagine a world that's really tiny compared to Earth – Mercury is just like that! It's the smallest planet, kind of like the little brother or sister of the other planets.

One of the coolest things about Mercury is how fast it zips around the Sun. It only takes about 88 Earth days to complete one orbit. That means if you lived on Mercury, a year would be shorter than three months on Earth! But a day on Mercury, from one sunrise to the next, is super long – it lasts 59 Earth days. So, if you were on Mercury, you'd have really long days and super short years!

Mercury looks a bit like our Moon. It has lots of craters, which are like big holes made by space rocks called asteroids and comets crashing into it. Because Mercury is so close to the Sun, it can get really hot, but it also gets super cold. This is because it doesn't have much air (which scientists call an atmosphere) to keep the heat in. So, during the day, it's hot enough to melt lead, but at night, it gets freezing cold!

One more fun fact: Mercury doesn't have any moons of its own. Most of the other planets do, but Mercury and Venus are the only ones in our solar system that don't have any moons.

Mercury also has a very unique feature called 'caloris basin' which is one of the largest impact craters in our solar system. This crater was created by a huge asteroid hitting Mercury long ago. It's so big that it could fit the entire state of Texas!

JOKE TIME!

Why did Mercury skip classes one day?

Because he had a very high temperature!

 **FACTS**

Extreme Temperatures: Mercury experiences the most extreme temperature fluctuations of any planet in our solar system. It can soar up to 430°C (800°F) during the day and plummet to -180°C (-290°F) at night, due to its lack of a significant atmosphere to retain heat.

The Smallest Planet: Mercury is the smallest planet in our solar system – even smaller than some of the moons.

Cratered Surface: Mercury's surface resembles the Moon, covered with craters due to collisions with comets and asteroids. The largest crater, Caloris Basin, is about 1,550 kilometers (960 miles) in diameter.

Ice on the Hottest Planet: Despite being the closest planet to the Sun, Mercury has water ice at its north and south poles. These ice deposits are found in permanently shadowed craters where the Sun's rays never reach.

Weak Atmosphere: Mercury has an extremely thin atmosphere, known as an exosphere, which is made up of atoms blasted off its surface by solar radiation. This means Mercury's sky is always black, even during the daytime.

The Iron Planet: Mercury has a disproportionately large iron core, which makes up about 75% of the planet's diameter. This is a much larger core relative to its size than any other major planet in the solar system.

4

MYSTERIES OF MERCURY

Mercury's Giant Core: One of the biggest puzzles about Mercury is its enormous metallic core, which makes up about 75% of its diameter. Was Mercury once a much larger planet that lost its outer layers from a colossal space collision? Or was it formed with such a big core from the start? This mystery challenges our understanding of how planets in our solar system were formed.

Weird Terrain: On the opposite side of Mercury from the massive Caloris Basin, there's an area known as the "Weird Terrain." This hilly, chaotic landscape is believed to have been formed by the shock waves from the Caloris impact. Studying this terrain will help to understand the effects of major impacts in shaping planetary surfaces.

Water Ice on Mercury: Mercury, though closest to the Sun, harbors water ice in shadowed polar craters, untouched by sunlight. This discovery, defying our expectations about water in the solar system, prompts a question: how did it arrive? Cometary impacts, perhaps, or another intriguing process?

Mercury's Thin Atmosphere: Unlike Earth, Mercury has a very thin atmosphere, or exosphere. Created by solar wind and micrometeoroids kicking up particles from Mercury's surface, it's a fleeting, transient atmosphere. Understanding how this exosphere is maintained despite the planet's proximity to the Sun can provide insights into atmospheric science on other planets.

Magnetic Field Mystery: Mercury's magnetic field is a real enigma. It's off-center, tilted, and northward, unlike any other planet in our solar system. This asymmetrical field challenges our understanding of planetary magnetism. How Mercury maintains this magnetic field despite its slow rotation is a question that intrigues scientists.

Venus

Distance from the Sun: Venus is about 108.2 million kilometers (67.2 million miles) away from the Sun.

Average Temperature: Venus experiences extreme temperatures, averaging around 464°C (867°F).

Size: Venus has a diameter of approximately 12,104 kilometers (7,521 miles).

Orbital Period: Venus completes an orbit around the Sun in about 225 Earth days.

Gravity: Venus's gravity is about 91% of Earth's.

Venus is a really special planet in our solar system, and it's the second one from the Sun. It's similar in size to Earth, which is why it's often called Earth's "sister planet." But Venus is very different from Earth in many ways!

One of the most interesting things about Venus is that it spins in the opposite direction to most planets in the solar system. This means on Venus, the Sun rises in the west and sets in the east - opposite to what we experience on Earth. Another fun fact is that a day on Venus (one complete rotation on its axis) is longer than a year on Venus (one complete orbit around the Sun)! A day there lasts 243 Earth days, while a year is only 225 Earth days. Imagine having a day that's longer than a year!

Venus is also known as the hottest planet in our solar system, even though it's not the closest to the Sun. This is because it has a very thick atmosphere filled with clouds of carbon dioxide and drops of sulfuric acid, which trap the heat. The temperature on Venus can reach up to a scorching 475°C (887°F) – hot enough to melt lead!

But don't think about visiting Venus for a summer holiday! Its surface is rocky and covered in thousands of volcanoes, some of which are still active. Plus, the air pressure on Venus is so strong, it would feel like being 900 meters underwater on Earth.

And just like Mercury, Venus doesn't have any moons. It's as if these two planets decided that they were already so interesting, they didn't need moons to make them more special! Venus really shows us how every planet has its own unique and fascinating story.

JOKE TIME!

Why did the astronauts struggle when they landed on Venus?
Because they faced a lot of pressure.

 **FACTS**

Extreme Surface Temperature: Venus has the hottest surface of any planet in our solar system, with temperatures reaching up to 465°C (869°F). This extreme heat is due to a runaway greenhouse effect caused by its thick atmosphere.

Rotates Backwards: Uniquely among the planets in our solar system, Venus rotates on its axis in the opposite direction to most planets, including Earth. This means on Venus, the Sun would appear to rise in the west and set in the east.

Crushing Atmospheric Pressure: Venus' atmosphere is composed mainly of carbon dioxide, with clouds of sulfuric acid, and has a pressure 92 times greater than Earth's – similar to the pressure found 900 meters (3,000 feet) underwater on Earth.

Volcanic Surface: Venus is covered with volcanoes and has a surface that is relatively young geologically, having been resurfaced by volcanic activity 300 to 500 million years ago.

No Moons or Rings: Unlike many other planets, including Earth, Venus has no moons or ring systems.

Similar Size to Earth: Venus is often called Earth's "sister planet" due to its similar size, mass, proximity to the Sun, and bulk composition.

MYSTERIES OF VENUS

Extreme Greenhouse Effect: Venus is shrouded in a thick atmosphere composed mainly of carbon dioxide, with clouds of sulfuric acid, creating an extreme greenhouse effect. This traps the Sun's heat, making Venus the hottest planet in our solar system with surface temperatures hot enough to melt lead. Understanding this runaway greenhouse effect can provide insights into climate processes on Earth and other planets.

Retrograde Rotation: Uniquely among the eight major planets, Venus rotates in the opposite direction to its orbit around the Sun (retrograde rotation). This means on Venus, the Sun would appear to rise in the west and set in the east. The reason behind this unusual rotation pattern remains a mystery and is a subject of scientific research.

Mysterious 'Snow' on Venus: High mountain peaks on Venus are covered in a bright substance that reflects radar. This 'snow' is not composed of water but likely to be metallic compounds such as lead sulfide and bismuth sulfide, precipitated out of the thick Venusian atmosphere.

Acid Rain and Metal Snow: Venus experiences a peculiar weather phenomenon. High in the clouds, there is acidic rain made of sulfuric acid. However, this acid rain evaporates before it hits the ground, and at the highest peaks, metal compounds condense out of the atmosphere, falling as 'snow.'

Mysterious Dark Streaks: Dark streaks in Venus' clouds, known as "unknown absorbers," absorb a large amount of ultraviolet light. These features have puzzled scientists for decades; they may be composed of complex sulfur or chlorine compounds, but their exact nature remains a mystery.

Earth

Distance from the Sun: Earth is about 149.6 million kilometers (93 million miles) away from the Sun.

Average Temperature: Earth has an average temperature of about 14°C (57°F).

Size: Earth has a diameter of approximately 12,742 kilometers (7,918 miles).

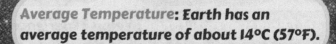

Orbital Period: Earth completes an orbit around the Sun in about 365.25 days.

Gravity: Earth's gravity is the baseline for comparison.

Earth is our amazing home in the vast universe, and it's the third planet from the Sun in our solar system. Unlike any other planet we know, Earth is just right for life. It's not too hot, not too cold, and has lots of wonderful things that make it special.

One of the best things about Earth is that it has lots of water - oceans, rivers, lakes, and even ice at the poles. This water is essential for all the plants, animals, and humans who live here. In fact, about 71% of Earth's surface is covered in water, which is why Earth looks like a beautiful blue marble from space.

Earth also has a day and a year that we are familiar with. A day on Earth, which is one spin on its axis, takes about 24 hours. This is what gives us daytime and nighttime. A year on Earth, which is one orbit around the Sun, takes about 365 days - that's why we have birthdays once a year!

Our planet has something very special called an atmosphere. It's like a big blanket of gases that surrounds Earth and keeps us warm. It also protects us from harmful space rocks and the Sun's rays. Plus, it's where we get the air we breathe!

Earth has one moon, which lights up our night sky. It's the only place beyond Earth where humans have walked. Our moon affects the oceans' tides and even some animal behavior.

So, while we learn about other planets, it's important to remember how special and unique our own planet is. Earth is our home, and it's up to us to take care of it so it can continue to be a wonderful place to live.

JOKE TIME!

What does Earth say to tease the other planets?

You guys have no life!

Water-Rich Planet: About 71% of Earth's surface is covered in water, and it's the only planet in our solar system where liquid water is known to exist on the surface, a crucial factor for supporting life.

Unique Atmosphere: Earth's atmosphere is composed of 78% nitrogen, 21% oxygen, and traces of other gases, including carbon dioxide and water vapor. This composition is vital for life, and Earth is the only known planet with an atmosphere rich in free oxygen.

Only Known Planet with Life: Earth is currently the only known planet in the universe to support life. The vast diversity of ecosystems and living organisms is unique to our planet.

The Goldilocks Zone: Earth is located in the habitable zone of the Sun, often called the "Goldilocks zone," where temperatures are just right to maintain liquid water.

A Large Moon: Earth's moon is relatively large compared to the planet itself. The Moon plays a significant role in influencing Earth's tides and stabilizing its axial tilt, which is important for the planet's climate.

Age: Earth is estimated to be around 4.54 billion years old, based on radiometric age-dating of meteorite material and is the densest planet in the Solar System.

MYSTERIES OF EARTH

Water's Mysterious Origin: One of Earth's biggest mysteries is where all its water came from. Was it brought here by icy comets from the outer solar system, or was it present in the dust and rocks that formed Earth? This question is crucial to understanding not only Earth's history but also the potential for life on other planets.

Earth's Core: We know that the Earth has a solid inner core and a liquid outer core, but much about the core remains a mystery. Questions about its exact composition, how it generates Earth's magnetic field, and the dynamics of its movements are still topics of ongoing research.

The Moon's Formation: The origin of the Moon is a topic of debate among scientists. The leading theory suggests a Mars-sized body collided with the early Earth, and the debris from this impact formed the Moon. However, there are still many unanswered questions about how exactly this process occurred.

Life's Origins: The origin of life on Earth is a profound mystery. While the basic chemical building blocks of life are understood, how these inanimate molecules combined to form living organisms remains one of the biggest questions in science.

Deep Ocean Mysteries: The deep ocean is one of the least explored parts of Earth. It holds countless unknown species and ecosystems. The extreme conditions of the deep sea, such as high pressure, low temperatures, and darkness, create unique habitats that we are only beginning to understand.

Mars

Distance from the Sun: Mars is about 227.9 million kilometers (141.6 million miles) away from the Sun.

Average Temperature: Mars has an average temperature of about -28°C (-20°F).

Size: Mars has a diameter of approximately 6,779 kilometers (4,212 miles).

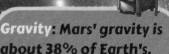

Gravity: Mars' gravity is about 38% of Earth's.

Orbital Period: Mars completes an orbit around the Sun in about 687 Earth days.

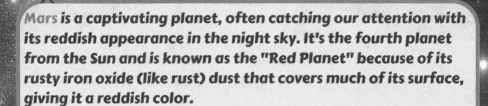

Mars is a captivating planet, often catching our attention with its reddish appearance in the night sky. It's the fourth planet from the Sun and is known as the "Red Planet" because of its rusty iron oxide (like rust) dust that covers much of its surface, giving it a reddish color.

Mars is about half the size of Earth, but it has some super cool features. One of the most interesting things about Mars is the largest volcano in our solar system, called Olympus Mons. It's so big that it's almost three times the height of Mount Everest, Earth's tallest mountain! Mars also has a gigantic canyon named Valles Marineris, which is over 4,000 kilometers long and much wider and deeper than the Grand Canyon on Earth.

A day on Mars is just a little longer than a day on Earth – it's about 24.6 hours. But a year on Mars, which is how long it takes to go around the Sun, is almost twice as long as a year on Earth – about 687 Earth days.
Mars has seasons like Earth because its axis is tilted, but they last longer because of its longer year. The planet has polar ice caps too, which can grow and shrink with the seasons. These ice caps are made of water and frozen carbon dioxide, which we call "dry ice."

One of the most exciting things about Mars is that it might have had water on its surface in the past, and scientists think it could have supported life a long time ago. They've found signs of dried-up rivers and lakes on Mars, which makes us wonder if there could have been living things there once.
Mars has two small moons named Phobos and Deimos. They're much smaller than Earth's moon and are thought to be captured asteroids.

JOKE TIME!

What type of music do they play the most on Mars?

Martian rock

Red Planet: Mars is often called the "Red Planet" due to its reddish appearance. This color comes from iron oxide, or rust, on its surface.

Water Evidence: Mars has signs of ancient rivers, lakes, and possibly oceans, although today it has no liquid water on its surface. The polar ice caps, made of water and carbon dioxide ice, indicate that water existed in the past.

Tallest Volcano: Olympus Mons, the tallest volcano and second-highest known mountain in the Solar System, is located on Mars. It stands about 22 km (13.6 miles) high, nearly three times the height of Mount Everest.

Thin Atmosphere: Mars has a thin atmosphere, composed mostly of carbon dioxide, with traces of nitrogen and argon. Its atmospheric pressure is less than 1% of Earth's.

Moons: Mars has two small moons, Phobos and Deimos, which are thought to be captured asteroids from the asteroid belt.

Potential for Life: Mars is a primary target in the search for past or present life outside Earth, due to its relatively hospitable past conditions.

Seasons: Like Earth, Mars has seasons due to the tilt of its rotational axis. However, a Martian year is almost twice as long as an Earth year.

MYSTERIES OF MARS

The Mystery of Martian Water: Mars has features like valleys and dried-up riverbeds that suggest it once had liquid water. How Mars went from a potentially water-rich planet to the barren landscape we see today remains a key question. Understanding this transformation could provide insights into planetary climate change.

Life on Mars: One of the biggest questions about Mars is whether it ever supported life. The presence of methane in the Martian atmosphere, seasonal changes in atmospheric methane, and organic molecules found in Martian soil are tantalizing clues in this ongoing mystery.

The Face on Mars: In 1976, a Viking I orbiter photo showed a formation that looked like a humanoid face. Later high-resolution imaging and analysis showed it to be a natural rock formation, but it sparked widespread public interest and speculation about ancient civilizations on Mars.

Phobos and Deimos' Origin: Mars has two small moons, Phobos and Deimos, which are thought to be captured asteroids. However, their origin is still debated. Some scientists speculate they might be fragments of a larger moon that was destroyed.

Methane Mystery: The intermittent presence of methane in Mars' atmosphere is puzzling, as it could potentially be produced by biological or geological processes. The Curiosity rover has made several detections of methane, leading to questions about its source and variability.

Jupiter

Distance from the Sun: Jupiter is about 778.5 million kilometers (483.8 million miles) away from the Sun.

Average Temperature: Jupiter has an average temperature of about -108°C (-162°F).

Size: Jupiter has a diameter of approximately 139,820 kilometers (86,881 miles).

Orbital Period: Jupiter completes an orbit around the Sun in about 12 Earth years.

Gravity: Gravity: Jupiter's gravity is about 250% that of Earth's (2.5 times that of Earth's).

Jupiter is a giant among planets and holds the title of the largest planet in our solar system. Imagine a planet so huge that more than 1,300 Earths could fit inside it! That's Jupiter for you, located fifth from the Sun and easily visible from Earth without a telescope, shining brightly in the night sky.

One of the most fascinating features of Jupiter is its Great Red Spot, a giant storm that's been raging for at least 400 years. This storm is so big that three Earths could fit side by side inside it. Imagine a storm that big!

Jupiter is known as a gas giant, which means it doesn't have a solid surface like Earth. It's made mostly of hydrogen and helium, just like the Sun. Because of this, if you tried to stand on Jupiter, you'd just sink into its clouds.

A day on Jupiter is the shortest of all the planets in our solar system. It spins on its axis very quickly, making a full rotation in just under 10 hours. This fast spin makes Jupiter bulge at the equator and flatten at the poles. But while its days are short, a year on Jupiter – the time it takes to orbit the Sun – is quite long, about 12 Earth years.

One of the coolest things about Jupiter is its many moons – it has 79 known moons! The four largest moons, known as the Galilean moons – Io, Europa, Ganymede, and Callisto – were discovered by Galileo Galilei in 1610. Ganymede, the largest of these moons, is even bigger than the planet Mercury.

JOKE TIME!

How does Jupiter hold up its pants?

With an asteroid belt!

FACTS

Massive Size: Jupiter is so large that it could fit all the other planets in the solar system inside it. It's over 1,300 times the volume of Earth.

Great Red Spot: One of Jupiter's most notable features is the Great Red Spot, a gigantic storm larger than Earth that has been raging for at least 350 years.

Short Days, Long Years: Despite its size, Jupiter has the shortest day in the solar system, rotating once every just under 10 hours. However, a year on Jupiter (one orbit around the Sun) takes about 12 Earth years.

Many Moons: Jupiter has 95 known moons, as of 1 November 2023, including the four large Galilean moons: Io, Europa, Ganymede, and Callisto.

Strong Magnetic Field: Jupiter has the strongest magnetic field of any planet in the solar system, about 20,000 times stronger than Earth's. This magnetic field creates bright auroras around the planet's poles.

Mostly Made of Gas: Jupiter is a gas giant made primarily of hydrogen and helium. It doesn't have a solid surface like Earth.

Rings: While not as famous as Saturn's, Jupiter has its own ring system, made up primarily of dust particles.

MYSTERIES OF JUPITER

The Great Red Spot: Perhaps Jupiter's most famous feature, the Great Red Spot, is a gigantic storm larger than Earth that has been raging for centuries. Understanding why this storm has persisted for so long and what keeps its energy up is a significant area of research.

The Metallic Hydrogen Mystery: Deep within Jupiter, under extreme pressure and temperatures, hydrogen is believed to exist in a metallic state, conducting electricity and creating Jupiter's powerful magnetic field. This exotic form of hydrogen is not found naturally on Earth and is a subject of intense study.

The Internal Heat Source: Jupiter emits more energy than it receives from the Sun, implying an internal heat source. The exact mechanisms of this internal heat production, whether residual heat from its formation or a result of its ongoing compression and gravitational contraction, are still being explored.

The Galilean Moons: Jupiter's four largest moons - Io, Europa, Ganymede, and Callisto, known as the Galilean moons - are worlds unto themselves, with unique characteristics like volcanic activity on Io and a subsurface ocean on Europa. Understanding these moons provides insights into the potential for life in the solar system.

Jupiter's Rings: Unlike Saturn's prominent rings, Jupiter's ring system is faint and mainly composed of dust. These rings were a surprising discovery, and their composition and formation mechanisms differ significantly from those of Saturn.

Saturn

Distance from the Sun: Saturn is about 1.4 billion kilometers (886 million miles) away from the Sun.

Average Temperature: Saturn has an average temperature of about -138°C (-216°F).

Size: Saturn has a diameter of approximately 116,460 kilometers (72,366 miles).

Orbital Period: Saturn completes an orbit around the Sun in about 29.5 Earth years.

Gravity: Saturn's gravity is about 1.1 times Earth's.

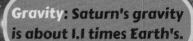

Saturn is one of the most amazing planets in our solar system, famous for its stunning rings. It's the sixth planet from the Sun and the second-largest, right after Jupiter. If you think of planets as a family, Saturn would be Jupiter's big, beautiful sibling.

The most fascinating feature of Saturn is its rings. These rings are made of ice, rock, and dust, and they stretch out into space for thousands of kilometers. But despite their size, the rings are quite thin, some places only about 10 meters thick. Imagine how they glitter like diamonds when the Sun shines on them!

Saturn is another gas giant, like Jupiter, which means it doesn't have a solid surface where you could stand. It's mostly made up of hydrogen and helium. Saturn is so light for its size that if you could find a bathtub big enough, Saturn would float in it!

A day on Saturn is pretty short. The planet spins on its axis very quickly, taking about 10.7 hours to complete one rotation. However, a year on Saturn is really long – it takes about 29.5 Earth years to orbit the Sun. So, if you lived on Saturn, you would have very long years and super short days.

One of the cool things about Saturn is its many moons. It has 146 moons that we know of (number still increasing!), with Titan being the largest. Titan is so big that it's even larger than the planet Mercury! Titan is special because it has a thick atmosphere and even lakes and rivers, but instead of water, they're made of liquid methane and ethane.

JOKE TIME!

Which planet is the richest?
Saturn, because it has so many rings.

 # FACTS

Iconic Rings: Saturn is best known for its spectacular ring system, which is made up of ice, rock, and dust. These rings are the most extensive and visible in the solar system, stretching up to 282,000 km (175,000 miles) from the planet but are only about 20 meters (65 feet) thick.

Many Moons: As of June 8, 2023, Saturn has 146 moons in its orbit, with Titan being the largest. Titan is larger than the planet Mercury and is the second-largest moon in the solar system, after Jupiter's moon Ganymede.

Least Dense Planet: Saturn has the lowest density of all the planets in our solar system. It's less dense than water, which theoretically means if there were a bathtub big enough, Saturn would float.

Fast Rotation: Saturn rotates very quickly on its axis, causing it to have a flattened shape. A day on Saturn (one complete rotation) lasts about 10.7 hours.

Interior and Heat: Saturn's core is likely composed of iron, nickel, and rock. Like Jupiter, Saturn emits more heat into space than it receives from the Sun, likely due to the gravitational compression of the planet.

Seasonal Variations: Like Earth, Saturn experiences seasons due to its axial tilt. However, each season lasts more than seven years because it takes Saturn about 29.5 Earth years to complete one orbit around the Sun.

MYSTERIES OF SATURN

The Composition of Saturn's Rings: Saturn's rings, made primarily of ice particles mixed with dust and other chemicals, have puzzled scientists for years. Their origin, age, and the processes that maintain their distinct gaps and structures are still not fully understood.

Hexagon on the North Pole: A persistent hexagonal cloud pattern on Saturn's north pole, each side longer than the Earth's diameter, is a unique atmospheric phenomenon in our solar system. The formation and stability of this hexagon, with its Earth-sized hurricane-like storm at the center, remain a mystery.

Mysterious Internal Heat Source: Like Jupiter, Saturn emits more heat than it receives from the Sun. This excess heat is believed to be due to the gravitational compression of the planet itself, a process known as Kelvin-Helmholtz heating, but the exact mechanisms are still being studied.

Saturn's Moons and Their Interactions: Saturn has 146 moons (number still growing!), each with its own unique characteristics. Titan, its largest moon, has a thick atmosphere and liquid methane lakes. Enceladus, another moon, has geysers that eject water into space, which then may feed into Saturn's rings.

Mystery of the 'Spokes' in the Rings: In the 1980s, Voyager missions observed strange radial 'spokes' in Saturn's rings, thought to be caused by the planet's magnetic field. However, their formation and transient nature are not well understood.

Uranus

Distance from the Sun: Uranus is about 2.9 billion kilometers (1.8 billion miles) away from the Sun.

Average Temperature: Uranus's average temperature is around -195°C (-320°F).

Size: Uranus has a diameter of approximately 50,724 kilometers (31,518 miles).

Orbital Period: Uranus completes an orbit around the Sun in about 84 Earth years.

Gravity: Uranus's gravity is about 89% of Earth's.

Uranus is a unique and intriguing planet in our solar system, known for its beautiful blue-green color. It's the seventh planet from the Sun and the third-largest in terms of diameter. Uranus stands out in the solar system for a few really interesting reasons.

One of the most remarkable things about Uranus is that it rotates on its side. While most planets spin like tops around the Sun, Uranus rolls along its orbit like a ball. This unusual tilt means that Uranus has extreme seasons. Each season lasts for about 21 Earth years, so a single year on Uranus, which is one orbit around the Sun, takes about 84 Earth years. Imagine having a winter or a summer that lasts for over two decades!

Uranus is often called an 'ice giant' because it has a lot of water, ammonia, and methane ice in its atmosphere. The methane gives Uranus its unique blue-green color, as it absorbs red light and reflects blue and green light.

This planet is quite chilly. The temperatures in the upper atmosphere of Uranus are some of the coldest in the solar system, dropping to about -224 degrees Celsius (-371 degrees Fahrenheit). Despite being so cold, Uranus has really fast winds that can blow at more than 900 kilometers per hour (560 miles per hour).

Uranus also has a ring system, though it's not as noticeable as Saturn's. Its rings are darker and smaller, made mostly of chunks of ice and rock. In addition to its rings, Uranus has 27 known moons, named after characters from the works of William Shakespeare and Alexander Pope. The largest of these moons are Titania, Oberon, Umbriel, Ariel, and Miranda.

JOKE TIME!

Why don't aliens visit Uranus often?

Because every time they do, they can't stand the planet's gassy atmosphere!

 **FACTS**

Sideways Rotation: Uranus has a unique rotation axis that is tilted over 90 degrees relative to its orbit. This means it essentially spins on its side, with its poles taking turns facing the Sun directly during its orbit.

Extreme Seasons: Due to its extreme axial tilt, Uranus experiences drastic changes in its seasons. Each pole gets around 42 years of continuous sunlight, followed by 42 years of darkness.

Coldest Atmosphere: Uranus holds the title for the coldest planetary atmosphere in the solar system, with minimum temperatures dropping to -224°C (-371°F).

Pale Blue Color: Uranus' pale blue color is due to the presence of methane in its predominantly hydrogen and helium atmosphere, which absorbs red light and reflects blue and green light.

Ring System: Uranus has a faint ring system, discovered in 1977. Its rings are composed of dark particles, making them less reflective and harder to see compared to Saturn's rings.

Composition and Structure: Uranus is categorized as an ice giant. Its interior is primarily composed of ices, such as water, ammonia, and methane, above a small rocky core.

Moons: Uranus has 27 known moons, with names inspired by characters from the works of William Shakespeare and Alexander Pope. The largest moons are Titania, Oberon, Umbriel, Ariel, and Miranda.

MYSTERIES OF URANUS

Sideways Rotation: Uranus has the most extreme axial tilt in the solar system, rotating on its side at an angle of about 98 degrees. This unusual orientation leads to extreme seasonal variations and is thought to be the result of a colossal collision with an Earth-sized object long ago.

Extreme Seasons: Because of its tilted axis, each pole gets around 42 years of continuous sunlight, followed by 42 years of darkness. This leads to some of the most extreme seasons in the solar system and affects its atmospheric dynamics.

Methane-Rich Atmosphere: Uranus's blue-green color is due to methane in its upper atmosphere, which absorbs red light and reflects blue and green light. However, the exact composition of the lower levels of its atmosphere remains largely unknown.

Uranus's Faint Rings: Uranus has a system of rings, but they are very faint compared to those of Saturn. They were unknown until 1977 and are composed of dark particles, which make them difficult to observe. The mechanism of their formation and maintenance is still a matter of research.

The Unexplored World: Uranus has only been visited by a single spacecraft, Voyager 2, in 1986. Many of its characteristics remain mysterious, and there is a growing interest in sending another mission to study the planet in more detail.

Irregular Moons and Formation: Uranus has 27 known moons, many of which have irregular orbits and are thought to be captured objects. Understanding the history and formation of these moons can provide insights into the early solar system.

Neptune

Distance from the Sun: Neptune is about 4.5 billion kilometers (2.8 billion miles) away from the Sun.

Average Temperature: Neptune's average temperature is around -214°C (-353°F).

Size: Neptune has a diameter of approximately 49,244 kilometers (30,598 miles).

Orbital Period: Neptune completes an orbit around the Sun in about 165 Earth years.

Gravity: Neptune's gravity is about 1.14 times that of Earth's.

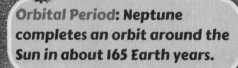

Neptune is a mysterious and beautiful planet, known for its striking blue color. It's the eighth and farthest known planet from the Sun in our solar system. Neptune is often called the "twin" of Uranus because they are similar in size and composition. But Neptune has its own unique features that make it really special.

One of the coolest things about Neptune is that it's the windiest place in our solar system. Winds on Neptune can reach speeds of over 2,000 kilometers per hour (1,200 miles per hour) - that's faster than the speed of sound on Earth! These strong winds whip up huge storms. The most famous storm on Neptune was the Great Dark Spot, which was as big as Earth, but it has since disappeared, showing how quickly weather can change on Neptune.

Neptune takes about 165 Earth years to orbit the Sun, so one year on Neptune is very long. However, a day on Neptune is pretty short - it rotates once every 16 hours. Because of its distance from the Sun, Neptune is a very cold place, with temperatures dropping to around -214 degrees Celsius (-353 degrees Fahrenheit).

This planet is also known as an "ice giant." It's made up of a hot, dense mixture of water, ammonia, and methane over a solid core. The methane in Neptune's atmosphere absorbs red light, which makes the planet appear a lovely blue.

Neptune has a faint ring system and 14 known moons. The largest moon, Triton, is unique because it orbits Neptune in the opposite direction of the planet's rotation. Triton is also one of the coldest places in the solar system, and it has geysers that shoot icy material into space.

JOKE TIME!

Why did Neptune break up with Mercury?

Because Mercury was too hot-headed, and Neptune needed some cool space!

FACTS

Farthest Planet: Neptune is the eighth and farthest known planet from the Sun in our solar system. It was the first planet located through mathematical predictions rather than through regular observation of the sky.

Intense Weather: Neptune has the strongest winds in the solar system, reaching speeds of over 2,100 kilometers per hour (1,300 miles per hour). It also has massive storms, with the Great Dark Spot being one of the most famous.

Deep Blue Color: Neptune's deep blue color is due to the absorption of red light by methane in the atmosphere, combined with an unknown component that gives the deep blue color.

Thin Ring System: Neptune has a system of rings, but they are very faint. They are made of dust particles mixed with ice particles and possibly coated with a carbon-based substance.

Ice Giant: Like Uranus, Neptune is categorized as an ice giant. Its atmosphere is primarily made of hydrogen and helium, with some methane, over a core of rock and ice.

Long Orbital Period: Neptune has an orbital period of about 165 Earth years. It completed its first observed orbit since its discovery in 2011.

Moons: Neptune has 14 known moons. The largest moon, Triton, is geologically active, with geysers of liquid nitrogen. Triton is unique because it orbits Neptune in a direction opposite to the planet's rotation.

MYSTERIES OF NEPTUNE

Extreme Winds: Neptune has the fastest winds of any planet in our solar system, reaching speeds of over 2,000 kilometers per hour (1,200 miles per hour). The mechanisms driving these incredibly high-speed winds in Neptune's upper atmosphere are not fully understood.

The Great Dark Spot: Similar to Jupiter's Great Red Spot, Neptune has a Great Dark Spot, which is a massive storm. However, unlike Jupiter's storm, Neptune's spots appear and disappear within a few years, leading scientists to question the underlying dynamics.

Internal Heat Source: Neptune radiates more than twice the energy it receives from the Sun. This suggests an internal source of heat, but the exact process of how Neptune generates and radiates this energy remains a mystery.

Methane Mystery: Neptune's deep blue color is due to the absorption of red light by methane in its atmosphere. However, the strikingly uniform color suggests additional unknown atmospheric components that influence its appearance.

Retrograde Moon Triton: Neptune's largest moon, Triton, orbits the planet in a direction opposite to Neptune's rotation, a retrograde orbit. This suggests that Triton may be a captured Kuiper Belt object. Triton's geologically young surface, nitrogen geysers, and thin atmosphere make it one of the most interesting moons in the solar system.

Neptune's Deep Interior: The composition and nature of Neptune's interior are largely unknown. It's believed to have a core of rock and metal, but the proportions and state of these materials are subjects of speculation and research.

Pluto

Distance from the Sun: Pluto is about 5.9 billion kilometers (3.7 billion miles) away from the Sun at its closest point, and about 7.5 billion kilometers (4.7 billion miles) at its farthest.

Average Temperature: Pluto's average temperature is around -229°C (-380°F).

Size: Pluto has a diameter of approximately 2,377 kilometers (1,477 miles).

Gravity: Pluto's gravity is about 6% of Earth's.

Orbital Period: Pluto completes an orbit around the Sun in about 248 Earth years.

Pluto, while no longer officially classified as a planet, remains an intriguing and beloved member of our solar system's family. It's known as a "dwarf planet" and is located in the Kuiper Belt, a region of space beyond Neptune filled with icy bodies and remnants from our solar system's formation.

Pluto is really small, especially compared to planets like Earth and Jupiter. It's so small that it's only about half the width of the United States! Because of its size, Pluto was reclassified from a planet to a dwarf planet in 2006, which was a big topic of discussion and debate in the world of astronomy.
Despite its size, Pluto has some big features. It has five known moons, with the largest being Charon. Charon is so big compared to Pluto that they actually orbit each other like a double system. The other four moons are Nix, Hydra, Kerberos, and Styx.

One of the most interesting things about Pluto is its heart-shaped region, officially named Tombaugh Regio, which was discovered by the New Horizons spacecraft in 2015. This region is a large, bright area made of nitrogen and methane ice. It's named after Clyde Tombaugh, the astronomer who discovered Pluto in 1930.
A day on Pluto is much longer than a day on Earth, lasting about 6.4 Earth days. And because Pluto is so far from the Sun, a year there is very long – it takes about 248 Earth years for Pluto to complete one orbit around the Sun.

Pluto is extremely cold, with temperatures dropping to around -229 degrees Celsius . Its surface is covered with mountains, valleys, plains, and craters. These features suggest that there might be some form of a subsurface ocean beneath its icy crust.

JOKE TIME!

Why did Pluto break up with the solar system?

Because it needed space – it just wasn't feeling the planetary vibe!

Orbital Characteristics: Pluto has a highly eccentric and inclined orbit. This means its orbit is more oval-shaped compared to other planets and is tilted compared to the solar system's plane. Sometimes, this orbit brings Pluto closer to the Sun than Neptune.

Surface Features: Pluto's surface is diverse, with large regions of frozen nitrogen and methane, mountain ranges, and vast plains. One of the most notable features is a heart-shaped glacier named Sputnik Planitia.

Size and Composition: Pluto is only about 2,377 km (1,477 miles) in diameter, making it smaller than Earth's moon. It's primarily composed of ice and rock.

Atmosphere: Despite its small size and distance from the Sun, Pluto has a thin atmosphere composed mainly of nitrogen, with traces of methane and carbon monoxide. This atmosphere expands as it approaches the Sun and collapses as it moves away.

Temperature: Pluto is one of the coldest places in the solar system, with surface temperatures averaging around -229 degrees Celsius (-380 degrees Fahrenheit).

Moon System: Pluto has five known moons: Charon, Styx, Nix, Kerberos, and Hydra. Charon, the largest moon, is so big compared to Pluto that they are often referred to as a double dwarf planet system.

Seasonal Changes: Pluto's elongated orbit and axial tilt lead to extreme seasonal variation. A season on Pluto can last for more than a century.

MYSTERIES OF PLUTO

Complex Geology: Despite its small size, Pluto has a surprisingly complex surface, with vast plains, towering mountains, and deep valleys. New Horizons images revealed a variety of terrains, including areas covered in nitrogen ice, rugged highlands, and regions that appear to be shaped by some form of erosion.

Atmosphere Variability: Pluto has a thin and tenuous atmosphere composed mainly of nitrogen, with traces of methane and carbon monoxide. This atmosphere expands when Pluto is closer to the Sun and collapses as it moves away, a phenomenon not fully understood.

Heart-Shaped Tombaugh Regio: One of the most striking features on Pluto is a large, heart-shaped region named Tombaugh Regio. This area has two distinct zones: Sputnik Planitia, a smooth, icy plain, and a rougher, mountainous area. The formation and composition of this region, particularly the icy plain, remain subjects of scientific inquiry.

Pluto's Moons: Pluto has five known moons: Charon, Styx, Nix, Kerberos, and Hydra. Charon, the largest, is so big relative to Pluto that they actually orbit each other in a double system. The interactions and origin of Pluto's moons are intriguing subjects of study.

Possible Subsurface Ocean: Research indicates that Pluto may harbor a subsurface ocean beneath its icy crust. The existence of such an ocean could have implications for the potential habitability of other Kuiper Belt objects.

Pluto's reclassification as a dwarf planet has not diminished its scientific importance. It continue to provide valuable insights into the nature of icy bodies in the outer solar system.

Sun

Distance from the Sun: As the center of our solar system, the Sun itself doesn't have a distance from itself. However, its average distance to Earth is about 149.6 million km (93 million miles).

Average Temperature: The Sun's surface temperature, or the photosphere, is about 5,500°C (9,932°F).

Size: The Sun has a diameter of approximately 1.39 million km (864,000 miles).

Orbital Period: The Sun doesn't orbit around another body, but it does rotate on its axis. Its rotational period varies from about 25 days at the equator to 35 days near the poles.

Gravity: The Sun's gravity is 28 times stronger than Earth's. If hypothetically, one could stand on the Sun

The Sun, the heart of our solar system, is a mighty star that holds everything from the smallest planets to the largest gas giants in its gravitational embrace. It's a G-type main-sequence star (a yellow dwarf) and is the single most important source of energy for life on Earth.

Despite being an average-sized star in the cosmic scale, the Sun is immense compared to the planets in our solar system. It's so large that about 1.3 million Earths could fit inside it! The Sun's enormous mass and gravitational power keep our solar system together, dictating the orbits of planets, asteroids, comets, and more.

The Sun is not just a glowing ball of light; it's a dynamic and complex star. It has a multi-layered atmosphere and a surface marked by sunspots, solar flares, and coronal mass ejections. These solar phenomena can influence the planets and space weather throughout the solar system.

One of the most striking features of the Sun is its 11-year solar cycle, during which the frequency of sunspots and solar flares waxes and wanes. This cycle impacts not just the Sun's appearance, but also has far-reaching effects, including on Earth's climate and satellite communications.

The energy produced by the Sun is the result of nuclear fusion reactions in its core, where hydrogen atoms fuse to form helium, releasing light and heat. This process has been illuminating and warming our solar system for about 4.6 billion years, and it's estimated that the Sun has enough fuel to continue for another 5 billion years.

JOKE TIME!

What does the Sun drink out of?

Sunglasses!

 **FACTS**

Enormous Size: The Sun accounts for 99.86% of the mass in the solar system. It's so large that about 1.3 million Earths could fit inside it.

Type of Star: The Sun is a G2V type star, a yellow dwarf. It's a middle-sized star and considered to be in the middle of its life cycle.

Energy Production: The Sun generates its energy through nuclear fusion. Every second, it fuses approximately 620 million metric tons of hydrogen into helium, releasing a tremendous amount of energy.

Distance from Earth: The Sun is about 93 million miles (150 million kilometers) away from Earth. This distance is referred to as an Astronomical Unit (AU), a standard measurement used to describe distances in our solar system.

Age and Lifespan: The Sun is about 4.6 billion years old and is expected to continue its main-sequence phase (normal mid-life stage for a star) for another 5 billion years.

Solar Activity: The Sun exhibits dynamic behavior, including sunspots, solar flares, and coronal mass ejections. This activity follows an approximately 11-year cycle known as the solar cycle.

Light Travel Time: Light from the Sun takes about 8 minutes and 20 seconds to reach Earth.

MYSTERIES OF SUN

Nuclear Fusion Core: *The core of the Sun is where nuclear fusion occurs, converting hydrogen into helium and releasing enormous amounts of energy. The exact conditions and processes in the core are subjects of ongoing study in astrophysics.*

Sunspot Cycles: *The Sun goes through an 11-year cycle of sunspot activity, known as the solar cycle. During the peak, solar flares and coronal mass ejections are more common. The underlying mechanisms driving these cycles are complex and not fully understood.*

Coronal Heating Mystery: *The Sun's outer atmosphere, the corona, is much hotter than its visible surface, the photosphere. Why the corona is hundreds of times hotter than the surface is a long-standing puzzle in solar physics.*

Solar Wind: *The Sun continuously emits a flow of charged particles known as the solar wind, which can have significant effects on planetary atmospheres and space weather. Understanding the solar wind's properties and interactions with the solar system is critical for space exploration and technology.*

Magnetic Field Reversals: *The Sun's magnetic field reverses polarity every solar cycle, approximately every 11 years. The process and implications of these reversals are important areas of solar research.*

Solar Neutrinos: *The Sun produces neutrinos, elusive subatomic particles, through nuclear reactions in its core. Detecting and studying these neutrinos helps scientists understand the fusion processes powering the Sun.*

Moon

Distance from the Sun: The Moon's distance from the Sun varies as it orbits Earth, but it averages about the same distance as Earth from the Sun, approximately 149.6 million km (93 million miles).

Average Temperature: The Moon's surface temperature can range from about -173°C (-280°F) at night to 127°C (260°F) during the day, due to its lack of atmosphere.

Size: The Moon has a diameter of approximately 3,474.8 km (2,159 miles).

Orbital Period: The Moon completes an orbit around Earth in about 27.3 days. This is also its rotational period, which is why the same side of the Moon always faces Earth.

Gravity: The Moon's gravity is about 17% of Earth's, meaning if you weigh 100 kg on Earth, you would weigh about 17 kg on the Moon.

The Moon, Earth's only natural satellite, is a constant and captivating presence in our night sky. It's the fifth-largest moon in the solar system and the largest relative to the size of the planet it orbits. Despite being much smaller than the Sun and the planets, the Moon holds a special place in both our sky and our cultures.

The Moon is more than just a celestial body to admire in the night sky; it's a key player in Earth's story. Its gravitational influence is responsible for the tides in our oceans and helps stabilize Earth's axial tilt, which in turn affects our climate.

The Moon's surface tells a tale of ancient cosmic events. It's covered with craters, mountains, and 'seas' or 'maria' – vast, flat plains formed by ancient volcanic eruptions. These features have remained largely unchanged for billions of years due to the Moon's lack of atmosphere and geological activity.

One of the most fascinating aspects of the Moon is its phases, changing from a thin crescent to a full circle, and then back again over a 29.5-day cycle. These phases have guided humanity in timekeeping and navigation since ancient times.

The Moon also holds the distinction of being the only other world in our solar system that humans have set foot on. The Apollo missions of the 1960s and 1970s brought twelve astronauts to the Moon's surface, marking a monumental achievement in human exploration.

A day on the Moon, from sunrise to sunrise, is about 29.5 Earth days. And interestingly, because the Moon rotates at the same rate that it orbits Earth, we only ever see one side of the Moon from Earth.

JOKE TIME!

Why did the Moon skip dinner?

Because it was already full!

 **FACTS**

Formation: The prevailing theory about the Moon's formation is that it resulted from a giant impact between Earth and a Mars-sized body, approximately 4.5 billion years ago.

Size and Distance: The Moon is about 1/4th the diameter of Earth and is about 384,400 km (238,855 miles) away from our planet.

Tidal Influence: The Moon's gravitational pull is responsible for the majority of Earth's tides. Its influence stabilizes Earth's rotation on its axis, contributing to a relatively stable climate.

Dark Side Misconception: There is no "dark side" of the Moon. All parts of the Moon receive sunlight at different times during its orbit. However, one hemisphere of the Moon always faces away from Earth, often inaccurately referred to as the "dark side."

Surface Conditions: The Moon has no atmosphere, no weather, and no sound. Its surface is covered in dust and rocky debris and is scarred with craters from meteor impacts.

Human Exploration: The Moon is the only celestial body beyond Earth that has been visited by humans. The first manned Moon landing was by NASA's Apollo II mission in 1969.

Phases and Eclipses: The Moon's phases are caused by its position relative to Earth and the Sun. It also plays a key role in eclipses when it passes between Earth and the Sun or when Earth casts its shadow on the Moon.

MYSTERIES OF MOON

The Moon's Formation: The prevailing theory of the Moon's formation suggests it was created when a Mars-sized body collided with the early Earth. This impact ejected material that eventually coalesced into the Moon. However, the specifics of this process and the Moon's subsequent evolution are still being studied.

Synchronous Rotation: The Moon rotates on its axis in about the same time it takes to orbit Earth. This results in the same side of the Moon always facing Earth, a phenomenon known as synchronous rotation or tidal locking. The reasons and mechanisms behind this are a significant area of lunar science.

Water Ice in Shadowed Craters: Recent missions have confirmed the presence of water ice in permanently shadowed craters at the Moon's poles. Understanding the quantity and distribution of this ice could be crucial for future lunar exploration and habitation.

Transient Lunar Phenomena: For centuries, observers have reported brief, mysterious flashes of light or color on the Moon's surface, known as Transient Lunar Phenomena. Theories about these flashes range from outgassing and impacts to electrostatic phenomena, but their exact nature is still not fully understood.

Mysterious Lunar Swirls: The Moon features enigmatic, sinuous markings known as lunar swirls. Their high albedo and unique patterns suggest they could be related to the Moon's magnetic field, but their exact nature remains a puzzle.

Halley's Comet

Distance from the Sun: At its closest approach, known as perihelion, Halley's Comet comes within about 88 million km (55 million miles) of the Sun. At its farthest, called aphelion, it is about 5.25 billion km (3.25 billion miles) away.

Average Temperature: The temperature of a comet like Halley's varies dramatically depending on its position in its orbit. Approx +200°C to -220°C

Gravity: The gravity on the surface of Halley's Comet is extremely weak due to its small mass and size. It's certainly much less than 1% of Earth's gravity.

Size and Composition: The nucleus of Halley's Comet is roughly 15x8x8 kilometers (9x5x5 miles) in size. It's composed primarily of ice, dust, and several organic compounds.

Orbital Period: Halley's Comet has an orbital period of approximately 76 years. It last appeared in the inner parts of the solar system in 1986 and is expected to return in 2061.

Halley's Comet, named after astronomer Edmond Halley, is arguably the most famous comet in human history. It is a 'short-period comet,' part of a group of comets that regularly return to the inner solar system. Its appearances have been recorded by different cultures around the world for millennia, each time weaving itself further into the fabric of human history and lore.

This celestial wanderer is known for its predictably spectacular returns to Earth's vicinity every 75 to 76 years, making it a once-in-a-lifetime event for many observers. It last graced our skies in 1986 and is expected to return in 2061.

Halley's Comet is a small body of ice, dust, and rocky materials, roughly 15 kilometers long and 8 kilometers wide. As it approaches the Sun, it heats up, causing the ice to vaporize and release gas and dust, forming a glowing head and a tail that can stretch for millions of kilometers.

The comet's orbit is highly elliptical, taking it far beyond the orbit of Pluto at its farthest and closer to the Sun than Venus at its nearest. This long journey through the solar system is a reminder of the dynamic and ever-changing nature of our cosmic neighborhood.

Observations of Halley's Comet have contributed significantly to our understanding of comets. Notably, it was the first comet to be observed in detail by spacecraft, providing valuable data about the composition and structure of cometary nuclei.

JOKE TIME!

Why don't the other planets play hide and seek with Halley's Comet?

Because it's only spotted once every 76 years!

Predictable Orbit: Halley's Comet is perhaps the most famous of all comets. It is best known for its predictable return to the inner solar system, which occurs every 75-76 years.

Long History of Observation: Halley's Comet has been observed and recorded by humans for millennia. Its earliest recorded sighting dates back to 240 BC in Chinese chronicles, but it wasn't until 1705 that Edmond Halley predicted its return, hence the name.

Composition and Appearance: Like other comets, Halley's Comet is composed of ice, dust, and small rocky particles. As it approaches the Sun, the heat causes the comet to release gases, creating a glowing head and a distinctive tail that points away from the Sun.

Tail Structure: The comet's tail can stretch for millions of kilometers in space. It actually has two tails: a dust tail and an ion tail, created by solar wind.

Size: The nucleus of Halley's Comet is relatively small, about 15 kilometers (9 miles) long, 8 kilometers (5 miles) wide, and perhaps 8 kilometers (5 miles) thick.

Cultural Impact: The appearance of Halley's Comet has been seen as an omen and has been recorded in many cultures throughout history. Its predictability has also made it a fixture in popular culture.

Next Appearance: Halley's Comet will next be visible from Earth in 2061, offering another generation the chance to witness this celestial object.

MYSTERIES OF HALLEY'S COMET

Origin and Age: One of the biggest mysteries about Halley's Comet is its origin and age. It is believed to have originated from the Oort Cloud, a distant area filled with icy objects at the edge of our solar system. Determining its exact age could provide insights into the solar system's formation, but it remains speculative.

Interstellar Connection: There is ongoing research into whether comets like Halley's could have brought water and organic compounds to Earth, potentially contributing to the emergence of life. The extent of this interstellar connection, however, is still a matter of debate and study.

The Comet's Core: The nucleus of Halley's Comet, which is the solid core of the comet, remains largely a mystery. Observations by spacecraft have provided some information, but understanding the detailed structure, internal composition, and how it has changed over successive orbits is still a challenge.

Mechanism of Outgassing: As Halley's Comet approaches the Sun, it heats up, and gases are released from its nucleus, creating its coma and tails. The exact mechanisms of this outgassing process, especially how it starts and stops, are not fully understood.

Long-Term Evolution: The long-term evolution of Halley's Comet, including how its orbit has changed over time due to gravitational interactions with planets and the Sun, is a complex and ongoing area of research. Predicting its future trajectory and changes is an intriguing aspect of comet studies.

Milky Way

Distance from the Sun to the Galactic Center: Our solar system, including the Sun, is located about 27,000 light-years away from the center of the Milky Way galaxy.

Size (Diameter) of the Milky Way: The Milky Way is estimated to have a diameter of about 100,000 to 200,000 light-years. It's important to note that the galaxy does not have a uniform shape, being a barred spiral galaxy, so these figures are general estimates.

The Milky Way, a name that evokes a sense of wonder and mystery, is the galaxy that contains our Solar System. It's a barred spiral galaxy, a majestic whirl of stars, gas, and dust, stretching about 100,000 to 150,000 light-years across. When we gaze up at the night sky, we are looking at a tiny fraction of the Milky Way's vast and intricate structure.

Our galaxy is home to hundreds of billions of stars, each with their own retinue of planets, moons, and smaller celestial bodies. At its core lies a supermassive black hole, Sagittarius A*, a colossal entity around which the entire galaxy rotates.

The Milky Way is just one of billions of galaxies in the observable universe, but it holds a special place for us as our cosmic home. Its spiral arms, named after the constellations they are seen in from Earth, such as Orion and Perseus, are sites of intense star formation and are speckled with brilliant nebulae, the birthplaces of stars.

One of the most striking features of the Milky Way, visible from Earth on a clear night, is the Milky Way's band - a luminous strip that stretches across the sky, formed from the dense concentration of stars in our galaxy's disc.

The Milky Way is also part of a larger cosmic structure known as the Local Group, a collection of more than 54 galaxies, including the Andromeda Galaxy, with which it is expected to collide in about 4 billion years.

JOKE TIME!

Why is the Milky Way so good at math?

It has millions of stars to count!

 **FACTS**

Spiral Galaxy: The Milky Way is a barred spiral galaxy, featuring a central bulge surrounded by four major arms and several smaller spurs. Our solar system is located in one of these smaller arms, known as the Orion Arm.

Vastness: The Milky Way spans about 100,000 to 150,000 light-years in diameter and contains an estimated 100 to 400 billion stars. The exact number is hard to determine due to the presence of dust and gas that obscure our view.

Supermassive Black Hole: At the center of the Milky Way is Sagittarius A*, a supermassive black hole with a mass equivalent to about 4 million times that of the Sun.

Galactic Collision: The Milky Way is on a collision course with the Andromeda Galaxy. This galactic merger is expected to occur in about 4 billion years.

Star Formation: The Milky Way continues to form new stars, particularly in its spiral arms where large molecular clouds of gas and dust can be found.

Population of Planets: Astronomers believe there may be billions of planets in the Milky Way, many of which could be Earth-like and potentially habitable.

Milky Way's Name: The name "Milky Way" is derived from its appearance as a dim, milky glowing band arching across the night sky. The term is a translation of the Latin "via lactea," itself derived from the Greek "galaxías kýklos" (milky circle).

MYSTERIES OF MILKY WAY

The Nature of Dark Matter: The Milky Way, like other galaxies, is believed to contain a significant amount of dark matter, an invisible substance that doesn't emit light or energy. The exact nature of dark matter and its role in the galaxy's formation and evolution remains one of the biggest mysteries in modern astrophysics.

The Supermassive Black Hole: At the center of the Milky Way lies Sagittarius A*, a supermassive black hole. The processes and dynamics surrounding this black hole, such as how it influences the galaxy's development and the way it interacts with nearby stars and gas, are areas of active research.

Galactic Formation and Evolution: The formation of the Milky Way, including how it evolved into its current spiral shape, is a complex puzzle. The process of galaxy formation involves the merging of smaller galaxies and the accretion of gas, but the exact sequence and timeline of these events are still being pieced together.

Star Formation Mysteries: The Milky Way continues to form new stars, particularly in its spiral arms. The mechanisms that trigger star formation, and why some regions are more prolific than others, are key questions in understanding our galaxy's lifecycle.

The Fate of the Milky Way: The future collision of the Milky Way with the Andromeda galaxy, predicted to occur in about 4 billion years, raises questions about the fate of our galaxy. The nature of this merger and its impact on the galaxy's structure and star systems is a fascinating topic of study.

Dark Matter

Creative interpretation of dark matter, web-like structure interconnecting galaxies and stars.

Approx 27% of the universe is made of this invisible dark matter.

Dark matter, an elusive and mysterious substance, pervades the universe, binding galaxies together and shaping the very structure of the cosmos. Despite being invisible and undetectable by conventional means, its presence is inferred through its gravitational effects on visible matter, light, and the large-scale structure of the universe.

Dark matter is thought to constitute about 27% of the universe's total mass and energy, far outweighing the ordinary matter that makes up stars, planets, and all living things. This unseen matter doesn't emit, absorb, or reflect light, making it truly dark and invisible to our current telescopes.

The existence of dark matter was first postulated in the 1930s by Swiss astrophysicist Fritz Zwicky, who noticed that galaxies in clusters were moving faster than could be accounted for by the visible matter alone. This led to the hypothesis of an unseen mass, providing the necessary gravitational force.

One of the most compelling pieces of evidence for dark matter comes from the observation of gravitational lensing, where the light from distant galaxies is bent around massive, invisible structures, presumed to be dark matter.

Despite its invisibility, dark matter plays a crucial role in the universe. It acts as a cosmic scaffolding, guiding the formation and evolution of galaxies and galaxy clusters. Without it, the structure of the universe would look very different, and our very existence might not have been possible.

JOKE TIME!

Why don't we invite dark matter to parties?

Because you can never tell if it shows up!

FACTS

Invisible Matter: Dark matter is called "dark" because it does not emit, absorb, or reflect any light, making it invisible to current astronomical instruments.

Massive Presence: Despite being invisible, dark matter is thought to make up about 27% of the universe's total mass and energy. In contrast, ordinary matter, which makes up everything we can see and touch, accounts for only about 5%.

Gravitational Effects: The existence of dark matter is inferred from its gravitational effects on visible matter, radiation, and the large-scale structure of the universe. It helps to explain the rotation of galaxies, the movements of clusters, and the apparent 'glue' that holds them together.

Not Made of Atoms: Unlike ordinary matter, dark matter does not consist of atoms. It is not made up of the particles that make up stars, planets, and all other visible objects in the universe.

Critical for Structure Formation: Dark matter is crucial for the formation of galaxies and other large structures in the universe. Its gravitational pull helped to pull together the first galaxies and influences the structure of the universe on the grandest scales.

Different from Dark Energy: Dark matter is different from dark energy. While dark matter appears to hold galaxies and clusters together, dark energy is thought to be responsible for the accelerated expansion of the universe.

MYSTERIES OF DARK MATTER

What is Dark Matter Made Of? Despite making up about 85% of the total matter in the universe, the true nature of dark matter is unknown. Theories range from weakly interacting massive particles (WIMPs) to undiscovered particles like axions, but none have been directly detected.

Dark Matter's Role in Galactic Formation and Structure: Dark matter is fundamental to the formation and structure of galaxies. It acts as a gravitational scaffold around which visible matter congregates and forms galaxies. Understanding how this process works in detail is a major focus of cosmology.

The Distribution of Dark Matter: The exact distribution of dark matter in the universe and within galaxies is not fully understood. While it appears to form vast halos around galaxies, the specifics of its distribution remain elusive.

Interaction with Ordinary Matter: Apart from gravitational effects, it's unclear if dark matter interacts with ordinary (baryonic) matter or itself in other ways. The search for non-gravitational interactions of dark matter is an active area of research.

Discrepancies in Theoretical Models: There are discrepancies between observations and theoretical models of dark matter, particularly on small scales (like the density profiles of dark matter in galaxies and the number of small satellite galaxies). These differences suggest that our understanding of dark matter physics might be incomplete.

Black Holes

> Depiction of a black hole, showcasing its event horizon and the surrounding accretion disk, with an effect of gravitational lensing.

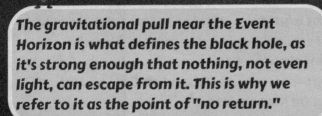

> The gravitational pull near the Event Horizon is what defines the black hole, as it's strong enough that nothing, not even light, can escape from it. This is why we refer to it as the point of "no return."

Black holes, the enigmatic titans of the cosmos, are objects of immense mystery and fascination. Formed from the remnants of massive stars, they embody extreme conditions where the known laws of physics are pushed to their limits. These cosmic phenomena are regions in space where gravity is so intense that nothing, not even light, can escape, rendering them invisible and elusive.

The concept of a black hole emerged from Einstein's theory of general relativity, which predicted that a sufficiently compact mass could deform spacetime to form a black hole. The first physical black hole ever discovered was Cygnus X-1, identified in the late 1960s.

Black holes can vary in size. Stellar black holes, formed from the gravitational collapse of massive stars, are common, while supermassive black holes, millions to billions of times the mass of the Sun, lurk in the centers of most galaxies, including our own Milky Way.

One of the most striking features of a black hole is the event horizon, a theoretical boundary beyond which no light or matter can return. This boundary marks the point of no return and is what most people think of as the 'surface' of a black hole.

Despite being invisible, black holes can be detected by their interaction with other matter. For example, if a star ventures too close to a black hole, it can be torn apart, emitting x-rays that can be detected by telescopes.

JOKE TIME!

Why don't black holes have friends?

Because they suck the life out of every party!

FACTS

Gravity Wells: Black holes are regions of spacetime where gravity is so strong that nothing, not even light, can escape from them. This intense gravitational pull is due to a large amount of mass being compressed into a very small area.

Event Horizon: The boundary around a black hole is known as the event horizon. It's the point of no return; once crossed, nothing can escape the black hole's gravitational pull.

Formation: Most black holes are formed from the remnants of a large star that dies in a supernova explosion. If the core's mass is more than about three times the mass of the Sun, it collapses to form a black hole.

Types of Black Holes: Black holes can be classified into three types based on their size: stellar black holes (formed by the gravitational collapse of a star), supermassive black holes (millions or billions of times the mass of the Sun, found in the centers of most galaxies, including our Milky Way), and intermediate black holes (a class with masses between stellar and supermassive).

Galactic Centers: Supermassive black holes are found at the centers of most, if not all, large galaxies. The one in the center of our Milky Way is named Sagittarius A*.

Singularity: At the center of a black hole lies the singularity, a point where matter is thought to be infinitely dense and the laws of physics as we know them cease to operate.

MYSTERIES OF BLACK HOLES

Singularity at the Core: At the center of a black hole lies the singularity, a point where matter is thought to be infinitely dense and the laws of physics as we know them break down. The nature of singularities and what happens within them remains one of the greatest puzzles in astrophysics.

Event Horizon Mysteries: The event horizon, the boundary beyond which nothing can escape a black hole, raises many questions. The behavior of matter and energy near the event horizon, and the nature of this boundary, challenge our understanding of physics, particularly at the intersection of quantum mechanics and general relativity.

Information Paradox: One of the biggest conundrums in modern physics is the black hole information paradox, which questions what happens to the information about objects that fall into a black hole. Does it disappear forever, defying quantum mechanics principles, or is it somehow preserved?

Formation of Supermassive Black Holes: The origins of supermassive black holes, found at the centers of most galaxies, including our own Milky Way, are still unknown. How these colossal black holes formed, particularly in the early universe, is a topic of intense study and debate.

Hawking Radiation: Proposed by Stephen Hawking, Hawking radiation suggests that black holes can emit radiation due to quantum effects near the event horizon. Detecting this radiation and understanding its implications for the fate of black holes is a significant challenge.

Orion Nebula

Depiction of the Orion Nebula, showcasing its vibrant and colorful cloud formations.

The Orion Nebula, also known as M42 (Messier 42), is a vast region of gas and dust where new stars are being born, located in the constellation of Orion.

The Orion Nebula, a dazzling and expansive cloud of gas and dust, is one of the most photographed and studied objects in the night sky. Officially known as M42, it resides in the Milky Way, nestled in the Orion constellation, and is a place where new stars are being born. This nebula is a window into stellar genesis, offering a glimpse into the complex process of star formation.

Visible to the naked eye as a fuzzy patch in Orion's "sword," the Orion Nebula is one of the brightest nebulae in the sky and can be seen without the aid of a telescope under good viewing conditions. It's a favorite among astronomers and sky watchers alike for its beauty and accessibility.

Spanning about 24 light-years across, the Orion Nebula is relatively close in cosmic terms, situated approximately 1,344 light-years away from Earth. This proximity makes it an ideal laboratory for studying the birth and early evolution of stars and planetary systems.

At the heart of the nebula lies the Trapezium Cluster, a young and vibrant group of stars whose intense ultraviolet radiation illuminates the surrounding gas, creating a spectacular cosmic scenery. These stars are so young that they represent the very early stages of stellar development.

The Orion Nebula is not just about star formation; it's also rich in protoplanetary disks – the building blocks of solar systems. These disks of gas and dust surrounding young stars are where planets, moons, and other celestial bodies are thought to form.

JOKE TIME!

What type of light does the Orion Nebula use to read?

Starlight !

FACTS

Stellar Nursery: The Orion Nebula is a massive star-forming region, one of the closest to Earth. It is actively forming new stars from its dense clouds of gas and dust.

Visible to the Naked Eye: Located in the Milky Way, lying in the Orion constellation, the nebula is one of the few nebulae visible to the naked eye from Earth under dark skies. It appears as a fuzzy spot in Orion's "sword."

Immense Size: The Orion Nebula stretches about 24 light-years across and is located approximately 1,344 light years from Earth. Despite its vast size, we only see a small part of a much larger cloud of gas and dust.

Bright and Young Stars: The nebula is illuminated by a group of massive, hot, young stars at its core, known as the Trapezium cluster. These stars are only a few million years old, very young in stellar terms.

Diverse Composition: The Orion Nebula contains a rich mix of gas clouds, new stars, protoplanetary disks, and various other astronomical objects. It's like a cosmic laboratory, offering insights into star and planet formation.

Part of a Larger Complex: The Orion Nebula is just one part of a much larger nebula complex known as the Orion Molecular Cloud Complex, which includes other famous nebulae like the Horsehead Nebula and the Flame Nebula.

MYSTERIES OF ORION NEBULA

Star Formation Processes: The Orion Nebula is a massive star-forming region, but the exact processes and conditions that lead to star formation within it are not fully understood. How stars of different masses form in such nebulae and the role of the nebula's complex gas and dust structures in star formation are key questions.

The Role of Stellar Winds: The Orion Nebula is home to massive young stars whose intense stellar winds and radiation significantly impact the nebula's structure and the star formation process. The mechanics of how these winds interact with the surrounding gas and dust are complex and not entirely clear.

Presence and Formation of Planetary Systems: The nebula is thought to be a fertile ground for the formation of planetary systems. The processes through which planets form in such environments, especially around massive stars, are still being explored.

Interaction with Surrounding Environment: The Orion Nebula is part of a larger complex of star-forming regions. Understanding how it interacts with its surrounding environment, including the influence of nearby supernova remnants and other nebulae, is important for a comprehensive picture of the region's dynamics.

History and Future Evolution: The Orion Nebula's past and future evolution, including how long it has been actively forming stars and what its eventual fate will be, remain speculative. Studying its evolution provides insights into the life cycle of similar nebulae across the galaxy.

Alpha Centauri

Depiction of the Alpha Centauri star system, focusing on the three stars: Alpha Centauri A, Alpha Centauri B, and Proxima Centauri.

Alpha Centauri is the closest star system to our Solar System, located about 4.37 light-years away from Earth. It consists of three stars: Alpha Centauri A and Alpha Centauri B, which form a binary pair, and a smaller, more distant red dwarf, Proxima Centauri.

Alpha Centauri, a shimmering beacon in the southern night sky, holds the title of our nearest stellar neighbor. This star system, a stone's throw away in cosmic terms, is a fascinating triplet of stars that beckon with both their mystery and proximity. Situated at a mere 4.37 light-years from Earth, it is a prime focus in the study of stars and potential interstellar travel.

This remarkable star system comprises three stars: Alpha Centauri A and Alpha Centauri B, which form a closely orbiting binary system, and Proxima Centauri, a smaller red dwarf. Each of these stars offers a unique perspective into stellar dynamics and characteristics.

Alpha Centauri A and B are sun-like stars, only slightly larger and smaller than our Sun, respectively. They orbit each other in a cosmic dance, showcasing the dynamic interactions that can occur in binary star systems. These stars serve as a comparative laboratory, providing insights into how similar or different sun-like stars can be from our own Sun.

Proxima Centauri, the faint red component of this trio, holds a special place in astronomical studies. It is not only the closest star to our Sun but also hosts an Earth-sized exoplanet, Proxima b, located in the habitable zone where liquid water could potentially exist. This discovery has fueled both scientific inquiry and imaginative speculation about the conditions on this distant world.

JOKE TIME!

Why don't they send time-sensitive messages to Alpha Centauri?

Because even at light speed, it's 4.37 years late!

 **FACTS**

Closest Star System: Alpha Centauri is the closest star system to our Solar System, located about 4.37 light-years away from Earth.

Three-Star System: Alpha Centauri is actually a triple star system, consisting of three stars: Alpha Centauri A, Alpha Centauri B, and Proxima Centauri.

Sun-Like Stars: Alpha Centauri A and B are similar to our Sun but with slight differences. Alpha Centauri A is slightly larger and brighter than the Sun, while Alpha Centauri B is slightly smaller and dimmer.

Proxima Centauri: Proxima Centauri, a red dwarf, is the closest individual star to the Sun and the least massive member of the Alpha Centauri system.

Proxima b: In 2016, an Earth-sized exoplanet named Proxima b was discovered orbiting in the habitable zone of Proxima Centauri. Its conditions are potentially suitable for liquid water to exist.

Future Exploration Target: Due to its proximity, Alpha Centauri is considered one of the prime candidates for future interstellar exploration and space missions.

MYSTERIES OF ALPHA CENTAURI

Planetary Systems: The quest to discover planets orbiting the stars of the Alpha Centauri system, particularly Earth-like planets, is ongoing. While Proxima Centauri hosts an Earth-sized exoplanet in its habitable zone, the presence of planets around Alpha Centauri A and B remains uncertain.

Stellar Interactions: Alpha Centauri A and B are a binary pair, orbiting a common center. Understanding the dynamics of this close binary system, including how they may affect each other's evolution and potential planetary systems, is a significant area of research.

Proxima Centauri's Flare Activity: Proxima Centauri is a red dwarf known for its flare activity. These flares can be intense, raising questions about the habitability of its orbiting exoplanet, Proxima b, and the conditions needed for life on planets orbiting red dwarfs.

Search for Additional Planets: While Proxima b is the only confirmed planet in the system, there is significant interest in detecting additional planets. The methods and technologies used to search for these planets, and what they might reveal about planetary formation, are areas of cutting-edge research.

Future Exploration: Alpha Centauri is a primary target for future interstellar exploration missions, given its proximity to Earth. The feasibility and design of these missions, including the challenges of interstellar travel, are subjects of ongoing study and speculation.

Exoplanets

Depiction showcasing a panoramic view of various exoplanets highlighting the diversity of planetary types that might exist outside our solar system.

Exoplanets are planets that orbit stars outside our Solar System. They come in a vast array of types, from gas giants larger than Jupiter to small, rocky worlds potentially similar to Earth, revealing the incredible diversity of planetary systems in our universe.

Exoplanets, the planets beyond our solar system, are hidden gems scattered across the vast tapestry of the cosmos. These distant worlds orbit stars far beyond our Sun, offering a glimpse into the incredible diversity of planetary systems in the universe. The discovery and study of exoplanets represent one of the most exciting and dynamic areas of modern astronomy, continually reshaping our understanding of where and how planets can exist.

Each exoplanet discovered so far is a world unto itself, with unique characteristics and conditions. From gas giants larger than Jupiter to rocky planets that may resemble Earth, these distant worlds come in an astonishing variety of types, sizes, and compositions. Some exoplanets orbit so close to their stars that their surfaces are molten, while others are icy, distant worlds, far from the warmth of their stars.

The first exoplanets were discovered in the early 1990s, but it was the Kepler Space Telescope that ushered in a golden age of exoplanet discovery, identifying thousands of potential exoplanets and confirming the existence of many. This flood of discoveries has revealed that planets are common in the galaxy, and potentially, the universe.

Among these exoplanets, a particular focus has been on identifying those in the 'habitable zone' of their stars—regions where conditions might be right for liquid water to exist, a key ingredient for life as we know it. The prospect of finding Earth-like worlds or even habitable environments beyond our solar system fuels both scientific research and the imagination.

JOKE TIME!

Why do exoplanets love astronomy jokes?

Because they're always out of this world!

First Discovery: The first confirmed detection of exoplanets occurred in 1992, with the discovery of several terrestrial-mass planets orbiting the pulsar PSR B1257+12.

Thousands Discovered: As of my last update, over 4,000 exoplanets have been confirmed in our galaxy, with thousands more candidates awaiting confirmation.

Diverse Types: Exoplanets come in various types, including gas giants, ice giants, rocky planets, and hot Jupiters (gas giants that orbit very close to their stars). There are even some that don't fit neatly into any category we see in our solar system.

Habitable Zone Planets: Many exoplanets have been found in their star's habitable zone, where conditions might be right for liquid water to exist – a key ingredient for life as we know it.

Different Sun Types: Exoplanets orbit a wide variety of stars, including sun-like stars, red dwarfs, and even pulsars. The characteristics of these stars greatly influence the potential habitability of the planets.

Planetary Systems: Many stars are found to have multiple planets orbiting them, similar to our solar system. The Kepler-90 system has as many planets as our own solar system.

MYSTERIES OF EXOPLANETS

Diversity of Exoplanets: Exoplanets exhibit an astonishing variety of sizes, compositions, and orbits, far beyond what is observed in our solar system. Understanding this diversity, particularly of "hot Jupiters" and "super-Earths," challenges existing theories of planetary formation and evolution.

Atmospheric Composition: Determining the composition of exoplanet atmospheres, especially of smaller, Earth-like planets, is complex. What these atmospheres are made of, how they evolved, and what they can tell us about the potential for life are key questions.

Habitability and Life: One of the most profound mysteries is the conditions required for an exoplanet to be habitable, and whether any harbor life. Factors such as planetary size, distance from their star, atmospheric composition, and stellar activity all play roles in habitability.

Formation and Migration: The processes by which exoplanets form and sometimes migrate from their original positions are not fully understood. The existence of gas giants very close to their stars (hot Jupiters) is particularly puzzling and suggests complex migratory histories.

Planetary System Dynamics: Many exoplanetary systems have been found with highly eccentric or closely-packed orbits, challenging our understanding of how planetary systems develop and maintain stability over billions of years.

Made in the USA
Coppell, TX
07 December 2023

25572097R00046